Collins
Very First
Spanish

DICTIONARY

Collins

HarperCollins Publishers

Westerhill Road
Bishopbriggs
Glasgow
G64 2QT
Great Britain

First Edition 2009

Reprint 10 9 8 7 6 5 4 3 2 1 0

© HarperCollins Publishers 2009

ISBN 978-0-00-730901-6

Collins® is a registered trademark of HarperCollins Publishers Limited

www.collinslanguage.com

A catalogue record of this book is available from the British Library

Printed and bound in China by South China Printing Co., Ltd

Acknowledgements

We would like to thank those authors and publishers who kindly gave permission for copyright material to be used in the Collins Word Web. We would also like to thank the Times Newspapers Ltd for providing valuable data.

SERIES EDITOR
Rob Scriven

MANAGING EDITOR
Gaëlle Amiot-Cadey

PROJECT MANAGEMENT
Susie Beattie
Genevieve Gerrard

DESIGN
Q2AMedia
Rob Payne

ILLUSTRATION AND IMAGE RESEARCH
Q2AMedia

Contents

a

airport
el **aeropuerto**

and
y
my brother
and *me*
mi hermano
y *yo*

adult
el **adulto**

alien
el **extraterrestre**

animal
el **animal**

after
después de
after *lunch*
después de *comer*

apple
la **manzana**

afternoon
la **tarde**
at three o'clock in the
afternoon
a las tres de la **tarde**

alphabet
el **alfabeto**

arm
el **brazo**

ask
preguntar
Ask *somebody.*
Pregúntale *a alguien.*

again
otra vez
Try **again**!
¡Inténtalo
otra vez!

ambulance
la **ambulancia**

b

balloon
el **globo**

banana
el **plátano**

baby
el **bebé**

basket
la **cesta**

bad
malo,
mala
bad weather
mal tiempo

bath
el **baño**

bed
la **cama**

bedroom
la **habitación**
(las habitaciones pl)

before
antes de
before three o'clock
antes de las tres

bag
la **mochila**

ball
el **balón**
(los balones pl)

beach
la **playa**

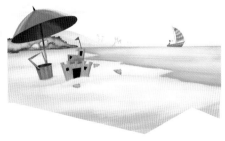

bicycle
la **bicicleta**

big
grande
*a **big** house*
*una casa **grande***

bird
el pájaro

birthday
el cumpleaños
(los cumpleaños *pl*)

black
negro, negra
*a **black** car*
*un coche **negro***

blanket
la manta

blue
azul
*a **blue** dress*
*un vestido **azul***

boat
el barco

body
el cuerpo

book
el libro

boot
la bota

box
la caja

boy
el niño

bread
el **pan**

brother
el **hermano**

butter
la **mantequilla**

breakfast
el **desayuno**

bucket
el **cubo**

butterfly
la **mariposa**

bridge
el **puente**

burger
la **hamburguesa**

bring
traer

*Could you **bring** me a glass of water?*

*¿Me podrías **traer** un vaso de agua?*

bus
el **autobús**

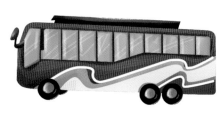

buy
comprar

*She's **buying** bread.*
*Está **comprando** pan.*

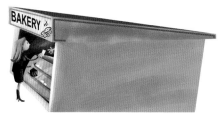

a
b
c
d
e
f
g
h
i
j
k
l
m
n
o
p
q
r
s
t
u
v
w
x
y
z

C

candle
la **vela**

castle
el **castillo**

cap
la **gorra**

cake
la **tarta**

car
el **coche**

cat
el **gato**

calendar
el **calendario**

card
la **tarjeta**

chair
la **silla**

call
llamar

Call this number.
Llama a este número.

carpet
la **moqueta**

cheese
el **queso**

chicken
el **pollo**

carrot
la **zanahoria**

child
el **niño,**
la **niña**

circle
el **círculo**

clock
el **despertador**

clothes
la **ropa**

circus
el **circo**

chocolate
el **chocolate**

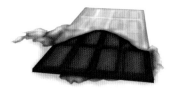

cloud
la **nube**

classroom
la **clase**

chopsticks
los **palillos chinos**

clean
limpio,
limpia
*a **clean** shirt*
*una camisa **limpia***

clown
el **payaso**

cinema
el **cine**

coat
el **abrigo**

computer
el **ordenador**

cow
la **vaca**

coffee
el **café**

cook
cocinar
I can cook.
Sé cocinar.

cry
llorar
Why are you crying?
¿Por qué lloras?

cold
frío,
fría

The water's cold.
El agua está fría.

costume
el **disfraz**
(los disfraces *pl*)

curtain
la **cortina**

come
venir
Come with me.
Ven conmigo.

countryside
el **campo**

d

daughter
la **hija**

dinner
la **cena**

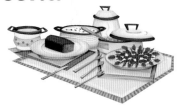

day
el **día**
*What **day** is it today?*
*¿Qué **día** es hoy?*

dinosaur
el **dinosaurio**

dad
el **papá**

dance
bailar
*I like **dancing**.*
*Me gusta **bailar**.*

dessert
el **postre**

dirty
sucio,
sucia
*My shoes are **dirty**.*
*Tengo los zapatos **sucios**.*

dictionary
el **diccionario**

dangerous
peligroso,
peligrosa
*It's **dangerous**!*
*¡Es **peligroso**!*

difficult
difícil
*It's **difficult**.*
*Es **difícil**.*

do
hacer
*What **are** you **doing**?*
*¿Qué **estás haciendo**?*

a
b
c
d
e
f
g
h
i
j
k
l
m
n
o
p
q
r
s
t
u
v
w
x
y
z

doctor
el **médico,**
la **médica**

door
la **puerta**

dream
el **sueño**

dog
el **perro**

dress
el **vestido**

downstairs
abajo
I'm downstairs!
¡Estoy abajo!

doll
la **muñeca**

drink
beber
Drink your milk.
Bebe tu leche.

dragon
el **dragón**
(los dragones *pl*)

dolphin
el **delfín**
(los delfines *pl*)

duck
el **pato**

draw
dibujar
Draw a house.
Dibuja una casa.

DVD
el **DVD**
(los DVDs *pl*)

a
b
c
d
e
f
g
h
i
j
k
l
m
n
o
p
q
r
s
t
u
v
w
x
y
z

e

egg
el **huevo**

evening
la **tarde**
*at six o'clock in the **evening***
*a las seis de la **tarde***

ear
la **oreja**

elephant
el **elefante**

every
todos,
todas
every day
todos los días

Earth
la **Tierra**

email
el **email**

easy
fácil
*It's **easy!***
*¡Es **fácil!***

exercise
el **ejercicio**

eat
comer
*I **eat** a lot of sweets.*
***Como** muchos caramelos.*

empty
vacío,
vacía
*The bottle is **empty**.*
*La botella está **vacía**.*

eye
el **ojo**

f

father
el padre

fire
el fuego

face
la **cara**

favourite
favorito,
favorita
*Blue's my **favourite** colour.*
*El azul es mi color **favorito**.*

fireworks
los **fuegos**
artificiales *pl*

fairy
la **hada**

family
la **familia**

find
encontrar
*I can't **find** my bag.*
*No **encuentro** mi mochila.*

first
primero,
primera
*the **first** day*
*el **primer** día*

fast
rápido
*You walk **fast**.*
*Andas **rápido**.*

finger
el dedo

fish
el **pez**
(los peces *pl*)

a
b
c
d
e
f
g
h
i
j
k
l
m
n
o
p
q
r
s
t
u
v
w
x
y
z

floor
el **suelo**
Sit on the floor.
Siéntate en el suelo.

flower
la **flor**

fly
la **mosca**

food
la **comida**

football
el **fútbol**

forest
el **bosque**

fork
el **tenedor**

fridge
el **frigorífico**

friend
el **amigo,**
la **amiga**

frog
la **rana**

from
de
a letter from my friend
una carta de mi amigo

fruit
la **fruta**

full
lleno,
llena
The bottle's full.
La botella está llena.

funny
divertido,
divertida
It's very funny.
Es muy divertido.

g

a
b
c
d
e
f
g
h
i
j
k
l
m
n
o
p
q
r
s
t
u
v
w
x
y
z

game
el **juego**

garage
el **garaje**

garden
el **jardín**
(los jardines *pl*)

ghost
el **fantasma** *m*

giant
el **gigante**

giraffe
la **jirafa**

girl
la **niña**

give
dar
Give me the book, please.
Dame el libro, por favor.

glass
el **vaso**

glasses
las **gafas** *pl*

glove
el **guante**

glue
el **pegamento**

go
ir
*Where **are** you **going**?*
*¿Adónde **vas**?*

goodbye
¡adiós!

grow
crecer
*Haven't you **grown**!*
*¡Cómo has **crecido**!*

goat
la cabra

grapes
las uvas *pl*

guinea pig
el conejillo de Indias

goldfish
el pez de colores
(los peces
de colores *pl*)

grass
la hierba

guitar
la guitarra

ground
el suelo
*We sat on the **ground**.*
*Nos sentamos en el **suelo**.*

good
bueno,
buena
*That's a **good** idea.*
*Ésa es una **buena** idea.*

a
b
c
d
e
f
g
h
i
j
k
l
m
n
o
p
q
r
s
t
u
v
w
x
y
z

15

h

happy
contento,
contenta
She is happy.
Está contenta.

head
la cabeza

hear
oír
I can't hear you.
No te oigo.

hair
el pelo
He's got black hair.
Tiene el pelo negro.

hard
duro,
dura
This cheese is very hard.
Este queso está muy duro.

hedgehog
el erizo

hairdresser
el peluquero,
la peluquera

helicopter
el helicóptero

hat
el sombrero

hamster
el hámster
(los hámsters *pl*)

have
tener
I have a bike.
Tengo una bici.

hello
¡hola!

hand
la mano *f*

16

here
aquí
*I live **here**.*
*Yo vivo **aquí**.*

hide
esconderse
*She**'s hiding** under the bed.*
***Está escondida** debajo de la cama.*

holiday
las **vacaciones** pl
*We're on **holiday**.*
*Estamos de **vacaciones**.*

homework
los **deberes** pl

horse
el **caballo**

hospital
el **hospital**

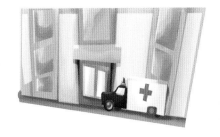

hot
caliente
*a hot **bath***
*un baño **caliente***

hour
la **hora**

house
la **casa**

hungry
*I'm **hungry**.*
Tengo hambre.

hurry up
***Hurry up**, children!*
*¡Daos **prisa**, niños!*

husband
el **marido**

a
b
c
d
e
f
g
h
i
j
k
l
m
n
o
p
q
r
s
t
u
v
w
x
y
z

17

i

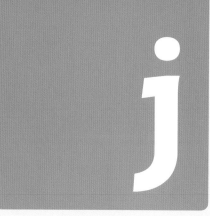

j

jigsaw
el
rompecabezas
(los rompecabezas *pl*)

a
b
c
d
e
f
g
h
i
j
k
l
m
n
o
p
q
r
s
t
u
v
w
x
y
z

ice cream
el **helado**

idea
la **idea**

insect
el **insecto**

island
la **isla**

jacket
la **chaqueta**

jam
la **mermelada**

jeans
los **vaqueros** *pl*

job
el **trabajo**

juice
el **zumo**
*I'd like some orange **juice**.*
*Querría un **zumo** de naranja.*

jump
saltar
Jump!
¡Salta!

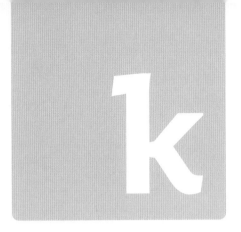

k

kind
amable
*a **kind** person*
*una persona **amable***

kite
la **cometa**

keep
quedarse con
*You can **keep** the book.*
*Puedes **quedarte con**
el libro.*

king
el **rey**

kitten
el **gatito**

knee
la **rodilla**

kiss
el **beso**
*Give me a **kiss**.*
*Dame un **beso**.*

key
la **llave**

knife
el **cuchillo**

kid
el **niño**,
la **niña**

kitchen
la **cocina**

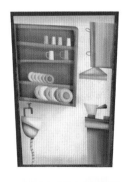

know
saber
*I don't **know**.*
*No lo **sé**.*

a
b
c
d
e
f
g
h
i
j
k
l
m
n
o
p
q
r
s
t
u
v
w
x
y
z

l

laptop
el **portátil**

leg
la **pierna**

lady
la **señora**

late
tarde
*I'm **late** for school.*
*Llego **tarde***
al colegio.

lemon
el **limón**
(los limones *pl*)

lake
el **lago**

laugh
reírse
*Why **are you laughing**?*
*¿Por qué **te ríes**?*

less
menos
*I've got **less** than him!*
*¡Tengo **menos** que él!*

lamb
el **cordero**

learn
aprender
*I'm **learning** to dance.*
*Estoy **aprendiendo** a*
bailar.

letter
la **carta**

lamp
la **lámpara**

light
la **luz**
(las luces *pl*)

like
gustar
*I **like** cherries.*
*Me **gustan** las cerezas.*

lion
el león
(los leones pl)

listen
escuchar
***Listen** to me.*
***Escúcha**me.*

little
pequeño, pequeña
*a **little** girl*
*una niña **pequeña***

live
vivir
*I **live** here.*
***Vivo** aquí.*

look
mirar
***Look at** the picture.*
***Mira** la foto.*

lose
perder
*I've **lost** my purse.*
*He **perdido** mi monedero.*

lost
perdido, perdida
*I'm **lost**.*
*Estoy **perdido**.*

loud
alto, alta
*It's too **loud**.*
*Está demasiado **alto**.*

love
querer
*I **love** you.*
*Te **quiero**.*

lucky
*You're **lucky**!*
*¡Tienes **suerte**!*

lunch
la comida

magician
el **mago**

many
muchos, muchas

*He hasn't got **many** friends.*
*No tiene **muchos** amigos.*

meet
encontrarse con

*I **met** my friend in town.*
*Me **encontré con** mi amiga en el centro.*

market
el **mercado**

make
hacer

*I'm going to **make** a cake.*
*Voy a **hacer** un pastel.*

meal
la **comida**

mermaid
la **sirena**

man
el **hombre**

meat
la **carne**

medicine
la **medicina**

mess
el **desorden**

milk
la **leche**

a
b
c
d
e
f
g
h
i
j
k
l
m
n
o
p
q
r
s
t
u
v
w
x
y
z

money
el **dinero**

monkey
el **mono**

monster
el **monstruo**

month
el **mes**
*What **month** is it?*
*¿Qué **mes** es?*

moon
la **luna**

more
más
*There are **more** girls than boys.*
*Hay **más** chicas que chicos.*

morning
la **mañana**
*at seven o'clock in the **morning***
*a las siete de la **mañana***

mother
la **madre**

motorbike
la **moto**

mountain
la **montaña**

mouse
el **ratón**
(los ratones *pl*)

mouth
la **boca**

mum
la **mamá**

music
la **música**

a
b
c
d
e
f
g
h
i
j
k
l
m
n
o
p
q
r
s
t
u
v
w
x
y
z

23

n

newspaper
el **periódico**

next
próximo,
próxima
the **next** street on the left
la **próxima** calle a la
izquierda

name
el **nombre**

need
necesitar
I **need** a rubber.
Necesito una goma
de borrar.

nice
simpático,
simpática
He's **nice**.
Es **simpático**.

neighbour
el **vecino,**
la **vecina**

night
la **noche**

noise
el **ruido**

nose
la **nariz**
(las narices *pl*)

nothing
nada
He does **nothing**.
No hace **nada**.

now
ahora
Do it **now**!
¡Hazlo **ahora**!

number
el **número**

123

nurse
el **enfermero,**
la **enfermera**

o

of
de
*some photos **of** my family*
*algunas fotos **de** mi familia*

old
**viejo,
vieja**
*an **old** dog*
*un perro **viejo***

only
**único,
única**
*my **only** dress*
*mi **único** vestido*

open
abrir
*Can I **open** the window?*
*¿Puedo **abrir** la ventana?*

other
**otro,
otra**
*on the **other** side of the street*
*al **otro** lado de la calle*

p

page
la página

paint
pintar
*I'm going to **paint** it green.*
*Lo voy a **pintar** de verde.*

paper
el papel

parents
los **padres** *pl*

passport
el **pasaporte**

people
la **gente**

pasta
la **pasta**

pet
la **mascota**

park
el **parque**

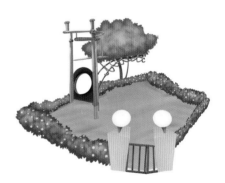

peas
los **guisantes** *pl*

photo
la **foto**

pen
el **bolígrafo**

piano
el **piano**

party
la **fiesta**

pencil
el **lápiz**
(los lápices *pl*)

picnic
el **picnic**

plane
el **avión**
(los aviones *pl*)

pocket
el **bolsillo**

picture
el **dibujo**

plant
la **planta**

pocket money
la **paga**

plate
el **plato**

police
la **policía**

play
jugar
*I **play** tennis.*
***Juego** al tenis.*

pirate
el/la **pirata**

pizza
la **pizza**

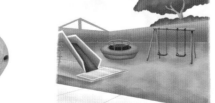

playground
los **columpios** *pl*

pony
el **póney**
(los póneys *pl*)

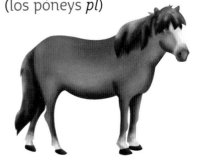

a
b
c
d
e
f
g
h
i
j
k
l
m
n
o
p
q
r
s
t
u
v
w
x
y
z

postcard
la **postal**

pretty
bonito,
bonita
a **pretty** dress
un vestido **bonito**

puppet
la **marioneta**

postman
el **cartero**

prince
el **príncipe**

puppy
el **cachorro**

pushchair
la **sillita de**
paseo

potato
la **patata**

princess
la **princesa**

pyjamas
el **pijama**

present
el **regalo**

a b c d e f g h i j k l m n o **p** q r s t u v w x y z

28

q

r

rainbow
el arco iris

queen
la **reina**

rabbit
el **conejo**

read
leer

I read a lot.
Leo *mucho.*

quick
rápido,
rápida

a quick lunch
una comida rápida

race
la **carrera**

ready
listo,
lista

Breakfast is ready.
El desayuno está listo.

radio
la **radio**

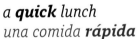

quiet
tranquilo,
tranquila

a quiet little town
un pueblo pequeño y
tranquilo

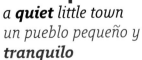

rain
la **lluvia**

red
rojo,
roja

a red T-shirt
una camiseta
roja

a
b
c
d
e
f
g
h
i
j
k
l
m
n
o
p
q
r
s
t
u
v
w
x
y
z

29

remember
acordarse de
*I can't **remember** his name.*
*No **me acuerdo de** su nombre.*

right
correcto, correcta
*It isn't the **right** size.*
*No es la talla **correcta**.*

robot
el robot
(los robots *pl*)

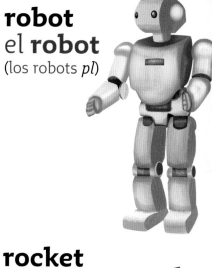

restaurant
el restaurante

ring
el anillo

rocket
el cohete

rice
el arroz

river
el río

room
la habitación
(las habitaciones *pl*)

rich
rico, rica
*He's very **rich**.*
*Es muy **rico**.*

road
la carretera

run
correr
Run!
¡Corre!

a b c d e f g h i j k l m n o p q **r** s t u v w x y z

S

sad
triste
*Don't be **sad**.*
*No estés **triste**.*

same
mismo,
misma
*They're in the **same** class.*
*Éstan en la **misma** clase.*

sand
la arena

sandwich
el **sándwich**
(los sándwiches *pl*)

say
decir
*What **did you say**?*
*¿Qué **dijiste**?*

school
el **colegio**

scissors
las **tijeras** *pl*

sea
el **mar**

second
segundo,
segunda

see
ver
*I **can see** her car.*
***Veo** su coche.*

sell
vender
*He's **selling** his bike.*
***Vende** su bici.*

a
b
c
d
e
f
g
h
i
j
k
l
m
n
o
p
q
r
s
t
u
v
w
x
y
z

send
enviar
Send me an email.
Envíame un email.

shadow
la sombra

sheep
la oveja

shirt
la camisa

shoe
el zapato

shop
la tienda

shorts
los pantalones cortos pl

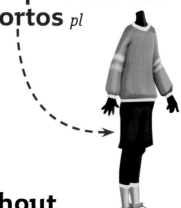

shout
gritar
Don't **shout**, children!
¡Niños, no **gritéis**!

show
enseñar
Show me the photos.
Enséñame las fotos.

shower
la ducha

sick
enfermo, enferma
He is **sick**.
Está **enfermo**.

sing
cantar
I sing in the choir.
Canto en el coro.

sister
la hermana

sit
sentarse
Can I sit here?
¿Puedo sentarme aquí?

sleep
dormir
My cat sleeps in a box.
Mi gato duerme en una caja.

snail
el caracol

snake
la serpiente

slow
lento,
lenta
The tortoise is very slow.
La tortuga es muy lenta.

skin
la piel

snow
la nieve

skirt
la falda

smell
oler
Mmm, that smells good!
¡Mmm, qué bien huele eso!

snowman
el muñeco de nieve

sky
el cielo

smile
la sonrisa

soap
el jabón

sock
el **calcetín**
(los calcetines *pl*)

soup
la **sopa**

spoon
la **cuchara**

sport
el **deporte**

sofa
el **sofá**

spaceship
la **nave espacial**

square
el **cuadrado**

son
el **hijo**

speak
hablar
Do you speak English?
*¿**Hablas*** inglés?*

stairs
la **escalera**

spider
la **araña**

sorry
¡**Lo siento**!

star
la **estrella**

station
la **estación**
(las estaciones *pl*)

stick
pegar
Stick it onto the paper.
Pégalo en el papel.

sticker
la **pegatina**

stone
la **piedra**

stop
parar
Stop, that's enough!
¡Para, ya basta!

story
la **historia**

street
la **calle**

strong
fuerte
She's very strong.
Es muy fuerte.

sun
el **sol**

supermarket
el **supermercado**

surprise
la **sorpresa**
What a surprise!
¡Vaya sorpresa!

swim
nadar
I can swim.
Sé nadar.

swimming pool
la **piscina**

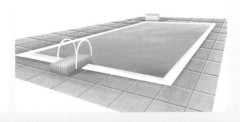

tall
alto, alta

*a very **tall** building*
*un edificio muy **alto***

telephone
el **teléfono**

table
la **mesa**

television
la **televisión**

take
coger

***Take** a card.*
***Coge** una carta.*

taxi
el **taxi**

text message
el **mensaje de texto**

tea
el **té**

talk
hablar

*You **talk** too much.*
__Hablas__ demasiado.

teddy bear
el **osito de peluche**

thank you
gracias

a b c d e f g h i j k l m n o p q r s **t** u v w x y z

think
pensar
*What **are** you **thinking** about?*
*¿En qué **estás pensando**?*

tired
cansado, cansada
*I'm **tired**.*
*Estoy **cansado**.*

toilet
el servicio

tomato
el tomate

third
tercero, tercera
*the **third** prize*
*el **tercer** premio*

toast
las tostadas pl

tomorrow
mañana
*See you **tomorrow**!*
*¡Hasta **mañana**!*

today
hoy
*It's Monday **today**.*
***Hoy** es lunes.*

tie
la corbata

tooth
el diente

together
juntos, juntas

tiger
el tigre

toothbrush
el cepillo de dientes

a b c d e f g h i j k l m n o p q r s **t** u v w x y z

toothpaste
la **pasta de dientes**

toy
el **juguete**

tree
el **árbol**

tortoise
la **tortuga**

tractor
el **tractor**

triangle
el **triángulo**

towel
la **toalla**

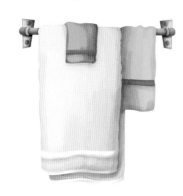

trousers
los **pantalones** *pl*

train
el **tren**

town
la **ciudad**

treasure
el **tesoro**

T-shirt
la **camiseta**

a b c d e f g h i j k l m n o p q r s **t** u v w x y z

u

up
arriba
*The cat is **up** on the roof.*
*El gato está **arriba** en el tejado.*

very
muy
very small
muy pequeño

umbrella
el **paraguas**
(los paraguas *pl*)

upstairs
arriba

vet
el **veterinario**,
la **veterinaria**

understand
entender
*I don't **understand**.*
*No **entiendo**.*

video game
el **videojuego**

v

uniform
el **uniforme**

visit
visitar
*We're going to **visit** the castle.*
*Vamos a **visitar** el castillo.*

vanilla
la **vainilla**
a **vanilla** ice cream
un helado de **vainilla**

vegetable
la **verdura**

wait
esperar
Wait for me!
¡Espérame!

wake up
despertarse
Wake up!
¡Despiértate!

walk
caminar
He walks fast.
Camina rápido.

wall
la pared
There are posters on the **wall**.
Hay pósters en la **pared**.

want
querer
Do you want some cake?
¿Quieres un poco
de tarta?

warm
caliente
warm water
agua **caliente**

wash
lavar
Wash your hands!
¡Lávate las manos!

watch
el reloj

water
el agua f

wave
la ola

wear
llevar
He's **wearing** a hat.
Lleva un sombrero.

webcam
la webcam
(las webcams *pl*)

website
el sitio web

week
la semana
*I play football every **week**.*
*Juego al fútbol todas las **semanas**.*

weekend
el fin de semana
*I play tennis at the **weekend**.*
*Juego al tenis el **fin de semana**.*

welcome
bienvenido

well
bien
*She played **well**.*
*Jugó **bien**.*

wheelchair
la silla de ruedas

white
blanco, blanca
*My shirt is **white**.*
*Mi camisa es **blanca**.*

wife
la mujer

wild
salvaje
*a **wild** animal*
*un animal **salvaje***

win
ganar
*I always **win**.*
*Siempre **gano**.*

wind
el viento

window
la ventana

a
b
c
d
e
f
g
h
i
j
k
l
m
n
o
p
q
r
s
t
u
v
w
x
y
z

winner
el **ganador**,
la **ganadora**

wolf
el **lobo**

world
el **mundo**

woman
la **mujer**

write
escribir
*I'm **writing** to my friend.*
*Le **estoy escribiendo** a*
mi amigo.

witch
la **bruja**

word
la **palabra**

with
con
*Come **with** me.*
*Ven **con**migo.*

work
trabajar
*She **works** in a bank.*
***Trabaja** en un banco.*

wrong
incorrecto,
incorrecta
*This answer is **wrong**.*
*Esta respuesta es **incorrecta**.*

without
sin
***without** a coat*
***sin** abrigo*

a
b
c
d
e
f
g
h
i
j
k
l
m
n
o
p
q
r
s
t
u
v
w
x
y
z

x

y

young
joven
(jóvenes *pl*)
*She's **young**.*
*Es **joven**.*

X-ray
la **radiografía**

year
el **año**
*I'm seven **years** old.*
*Tengo siete **años**.*

z

yellow
amarillo,
amarilla
I'm wearing
***yellow** shorts.*
Llevo unos
pantalones
*cortos **amarillos**.*

zebra
la **cebra**

xylophone
el **xilófono**

yesterday
ayer
*I was late **yesterday**.*
***Ayer** llegué tarde.*

zoo
el **zoo**

Los animales
Animals

el **gato**
cat

el **cocodrilo**
crocodile

la **cebra**
zebra

el **elefante**
elephant

la **serpiente**
snake

el **pingüino**
penguin

44   la **jirafa**
giraffe

el **lobo**
wolf

el **lagarto**
lizard

el **caballo**
horse

la **vaca**
cow

el **perro**
dog

el **león**
lion

el **hipopótamo**
hippo

el **panda**
panda

el **tigre**
tiger

el **pájaro**
bird

el **conejo**
rabbit

el **pez**
fish

la **oveja**
sheep

el **mono**
monkey

el **canguro**
kangaroo

45

La ciudad
Town

la **panadería**
bakery

el **banco**
bank

el **supermercado**
supermarket

la **calle**
street

la **tienda**
shop

el **hospital**
hospital

la **estación**
station

la **oficina de correos**
post office

el **parque**
park

el **avión**
plane

el **autobús**
bus

el **tren**
train

el **coche**
car

la **bici**
bike

el **restaurante**
restaurant

el **cine**
cinema

el **museo**
museum

la **acera**
pavement

el **mercado**
market

47

El colegio
School

la **pluma**
pen

la **regla**
ruler

el **alumno**
pupil

la **cartera**
schoolbag

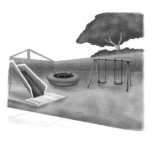

el **patio de recreo**
playground

el **tobogán**
slide

el **tiovivo**
roundabout

el **columpio**
swing

la **clase**
classroom

la **goma**
rubber

el **lápiz**
pencil

el **cuaderno**
exercise book

el **estuche**
pencil case

el **sacapuntas**
sharpener

el **póster**
poster

la **silla**
chair

el **ordenador**
computer

la **mesa**
desk

el **armario**
cupboard

la **pizarra electrónica interactiva**
interactive whiteboard

el **maestro** 49
teacher

La casa
House

el **desván**
attic

el **garaje**
garage

el **jardín**
garden

la **habitación**
bedroom

el **comedor**
dining room

el **cuarto de baño**
bathroom

la **escalera**
stairs

el **salón**
living room

el **tejado**
roof

la **cocina**
kitchen

el **despacho**
study

la **puerta**
door

la **ventana**
window

La habitación
Bedroom

el **despertador**
alarm clock

la **cama**
bed

el **juguete**
toy

el **ordenador**
computer

el **reproductor de CDs**
CD player

la **mesilla de noche**
bedside table

la **cómoda**
chest of drawers

la **librería**
bookshelf

las **cortinas**
curtains

el **armario**
wardrobe

la **lámpara**
lamp

el **espejo**
mirror

el **pijama**
pyjamas

la **almohada**
pillow

el **edredón**
duvet

las **zapatillas**
slippers

la **mesa**
desk

51

La comida
Food

las **patatas fritas**
crisps

la **galleta**
biscuit

el **agua** *f*
water

el **plato**
plate

la **taza**
cup

el **cuchillo**
knife

el **tenedor**
fork

la **cuchara**
spoon

la **manzana**
apple

la **naranja**
orange

las **zanahorias**
carrots

la **ensalada**
salad

52

la **mantequilla**
butter

el **queso**
cheese

las **patatas fritas**
chips

el **helado**
ice cream

el **pan**
bread

la **hamburguesa**
burger

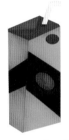
el **pollo**
chicken

el **zumo de fruta**
fruit juice

la **leche**
milk

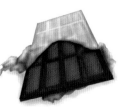
el **chocolate**
chocolate

la **pasta**
pasta

el **sándwich**
sandwich

la **pizza**
pizza

el **arroz**
rice

53

¡Feliz cumpleaños!
Happy birthday!

la **tarta**
cake

la **amiga**
friend

el amigo
friend

la **abuela**
grandma

el **abuelo**
granddad

las **patatas fritas**
crisps

la **limonada**
lemonade

el globo
balloon

la cámara
camera

la vela
candle

el papá
dad

la mamá
mum

la hermana
sister

el hermano
brother

el regalo
present

los caramelos
sweets

El cuerpo
Body

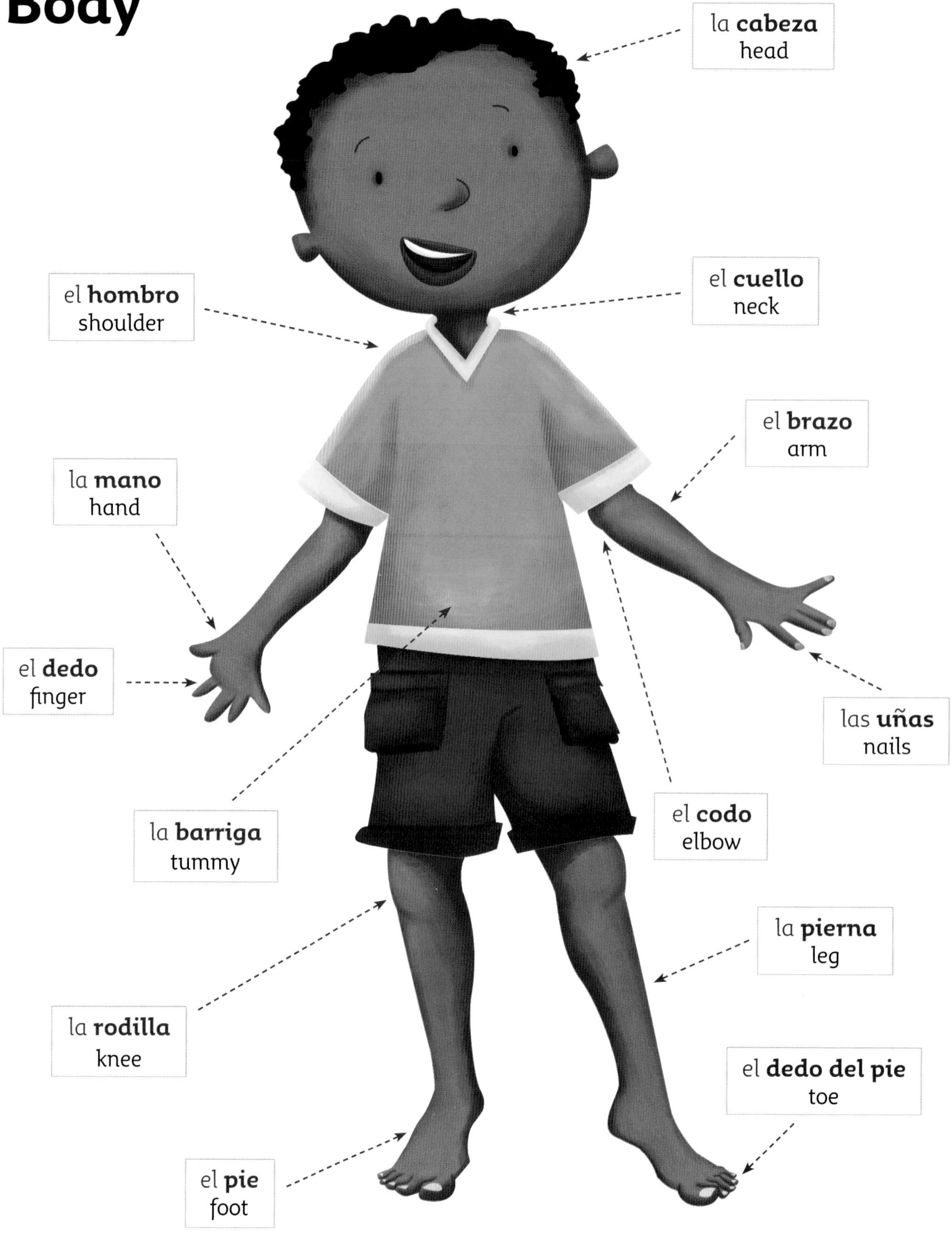

la **cabeza**
head

el **cuello**
neck

el **hombro**
shoulder

el **brazo**
arm

la **mano**
hand

el **dedo**
finger

las **uñas**
nails

la **barriga**
tummy

el **codo**
elbow

la **pierna**
leg

la **rodilla**
knee

el **dedo del pie**
toe

el **pie**
foot

La cara
Face

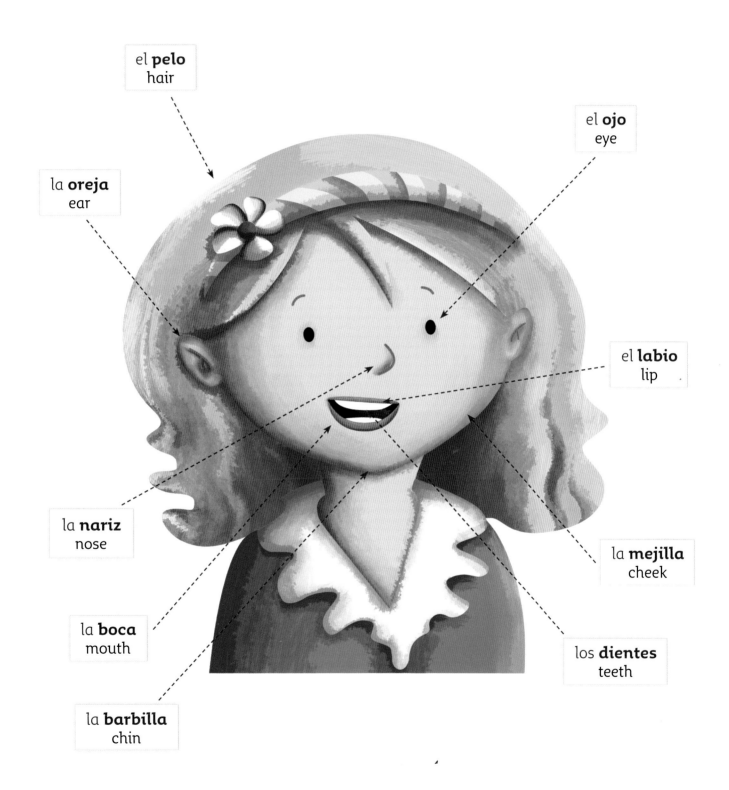

el **pelo**
hair

el **ojo**
eye

la **oreja**
ear

el **labio**
lip

la **nariz**
nose

la **mejilla**
cheek

la **boca**
mouth

los **dientes**
teeth

la **barbilla**
chin

Los colores
Colours

negro, negra
black

azul
blue

marrón
brown

verde
green

gris
grey

azul marino
navy

naranja
orange

rosa
pink

morado, morada
purple

rojo, roja
red

blanco, blanca
white

amarillo, amarilla
yellow

La ropa
Clothes

la **sudadera**
sweatshirt

el **vestido**
dress

la **chaqueta**
jacket

los **vaqueros**
jeans

la **bufanda**
scarf

los **guantes** *mpl*
gloves

el **abrigo**
coat

el **jersey**
jumper

los **zapatos**
shoes

la **camisa**
shirt

los **calcetines**
socks

la **gorra**
cap

las **zapatillas
de deporte**
trainers

el **top**
top

las **medias**
tights

los **pantalones**
trousers

la **camiseta**
T-shirt

la **falda**
skirt

el **gorro de lana**
woolly hat

Las descripciones
Describing people

Tengo calor.
I'm hot.

Tengo frío.
I'm cold.

Tengo hambre.
I'm hungry.

Tengo sueño.
I'm sleepy.

Tengo sed.
I'm thirsty.

Estoy contenta.
I'm happy.

Estoy triste.
I'm sad.

Soy inteligente.
I'm intelligent.

Las conversaciones
Conversations

63

¿Qué te gusta hacer?
What do you enjoy doing?

Me **gusta**...
I like...

bailar
dancing

cantar
singing

tocar la guitarra
playing guitar

tocar el piano
playing piano

jugar al fútbol
playing football

montar en bici
riding my bike

jugar al baloncesto
playing basketball

64

ver la televisión
watching television

escuchar música
listening to music

pintar
painting

jugar a videojuegos
playing video games

dibujar
drawing

jugar al tenis
playing tennis

nadar
swimming

Los meses del año
Months of the year

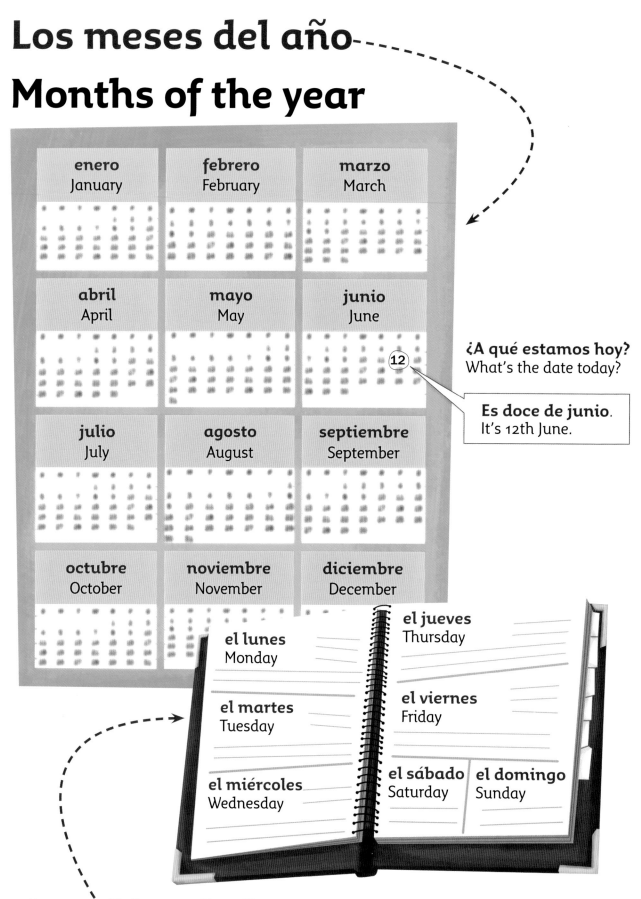

enero
January

febrero
February

marzo
March

abril
April

mayo
May

junio
June

julio
July

agosto
August

septiembre
September

octubre
October

noviembre
November

diciembre
December

¿A qué estamos hoy?
What's the date today?

Es doce de junio.
It's 12th June.

el lunes
Monday

el martes
Tuesday

el miércoles
Wednesday

el jueves
Thursday

el viernes
Friday

el sábado
Saturday

el domingo
Sunday

Los días de la semana
Days of the week

Las estaciones del año
Seasons

la primavera
spring

el verano
summer

el otoño
autumn

el invierno
winter

¿Qué tiempo hace?
What's the weather like?

Está nublado.
It's cloudy.

Hace frío.
It's cold.

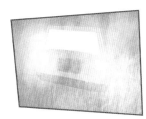
Hay niebla.
It's foggy.

Está helando.
It's icy.

Está nublado.
It's overcast.

Está lloviendo.
It's raining.

Está nevando.
It's snowing.

Hay tormenta.
It's stormy.

Hace viento.
It's windy.

Hace calor.
It's hot.

Hace sol.
It's sunny.

Hace buen tiempo.
It's nice.

Los números
Numbers

0 cero	9 nueve	18 dieciocho	70 setenta
1 uno	10 diez	19 diecinueve	80 ochenta
2 dos	11 once	20 veinte	90 noventa
3 tres	12 doce	21 veintiuno	100 cien
4 cuatro	13 trece	22 veintidós	101 ciento uno
5 cinco	14 catorce	30 treinta	200 doscientos
6 seis	15 quince	40 cuarenta	250 doscientos cincuenta
7 siete	16 dieciséis	50 cincuenta	500 quinientos
8 ocho	17 diecisiete	60 sesenta	1000 mil

¿Qué hora es?
What's the time?

la una
one o'clock

la una y diez
ten past one

la una y cuarto
quarter past one

la una y media
half past one

las dos menos veinte
twenty to two

las dos menos cuarto
quarter to two

¿A qué hora ...?
What time...?

a las once y cuarto
at quarter past eleven

a mediodía
at midday

a la una
at one o'clock

a las seis
at six o'clock

a las nueve menos cuarto
at quarter to nine

a medianoche
at midnight

¿Dónde están?
Where are they?

El perro está **detrás** de la televisión.
The dog is **behind** the television.

El gato está **arriba** en el tejado.
The cat is **up** on the roof.

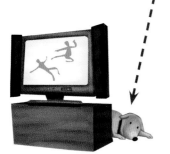

El coche está **delante** de la casa.
The car is **in front of** the house.

El ratón está **abajo** en el sótano.
The mouse is **down** in the cellar.

El pájaro está **lejos del** árbol.
The bird is **far away from** the tree.

El árbol está **cerca de** la casa.
The tree is **near** the house.

Va **de** la casa **al** colegio.
She is going **from** the house **to** the school.

Está **aquí**.
He is **here**.

Está **allí**.
She is **there**.

Espérame **fuera**.
Wait for me **outside**.

El gato está **en** la caja.
The cat is **in** the box.

Sale **del** jardín.
He is coming **out of** the garden.

Salta **a** la piscina.
He is jumping **into** the pool.

Está **dentro de** la casa.
She's **inside** the house.

El coche tuerce **a la izquierda**.
The car is turning **left**.

La bici tuerce **a la derecha**.
The bike is turning **right**.

El gato está **debajo de** la mesa.
The cat is **under** the table.

El perro está **entre** los dos gatos.
The dog is **between** the two cats.

El banco está **enfrente del** restaurante.
The bank is **opposite** the restaurant.

El perro está **en** el sofá.
The dog is **on** the sofa.

La panadería está **al lado del** supermercado.
The bakery is **next to** the supermarket.

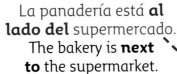

71

Nouns

Words such as 'apple', 'bedroom' or 'friend' are called **nouns**.

In Spanish, all nouns are either **masculine** or **feminine**. When you use a noun in Spanish, you need to know whether it is masculine or feminine, as this changes the form of other words used with it, like:

- adjectives (such as 'nice', 'blue', 'big') that describe it
- 'the' or 'a' that come before it

Nouns can be **singular** (meaning 'one') or **plural** (meaning 'more than one').

This dictionary shows you the Spanish words for 'the' (this can be **el** or **la** in the singular, and **los** or **las** in the plural):

- **Masculine** words are shown with the article **el** in front.

alphabet
el **alfabeto**

- **Feminine** words are shown with the article **la** in front.

apple
la **manzana**

- Plural words are shown with the article **los** or **las** in front, and are followed by a small '*pl*' for *pl*ural.

scissors
las **tijeras** *pl*

If a Spanish word ends in a vowel (a, e, i, o, u) then you add an **-s** to form the plural (1 gato - 2 gato**s**). If it ends in a consonant you add **-es** (1 animal - 2 animal**es**). If the plural is different to this (like '1 mouse – 2 mice' in English), then this dictionary will give you the plural of the noun, in brackets.

fish
el **pez**
(los peces *pl*)

Adjectives

An **adjective** is a 'describing' word (such as 'nice', 'blue', 'big') which tells you more about a noun.

In Spanish, they mostly come **after** the noun ('a car black'). but the spelling of the adjective changes depending on whether the noun it describes is masculine or feminine.

In this dictionary, you will find the **masculine** and the **feminine** forms, followed by an example:

black
negro, negra
*a **black** car*
*un coche **negro***

Verbs

Words such as 'eat' or 'make' are called **verbs** or 'doing' words. In Spanish the endings in verbs change much more than in English, depending on who is doing the action.

You don't always have to use **I**, **he**, **they** etc in Spanish as the endings tell you who is doing the action.

Here are a few of the main Spanish verbs:

tener	**to have**	**ir**	**to go**
yo **tengo**	I have	yo **voy**	I go
tú **tienes**	you have	tú **vas**	you go
él **tiene**	he has	él **va**	he goes
ella **tiene**	she has	ella **va**	she goes
usted **tiene**	you have	usted **va**	you go
nosotros/as **tenemos**	we have	nosotros/as **vamos**	we go
vosotros/as **tenéis**	you have	vosotros/as **vais**	you go
ellos/ellas **tienen**	they have	ellos/ellas **van**	they go
ustedes **tienen**	you have	ustedes **van**	you go

ser	**to be**	**hacer**	**to make, to do**
yo **soy**	I am	yo **hago**	I make
tú **eres**	you are	tú **haces**	you make
él **es**	he is	él **hace**	he makes
ella **es**	she is	ella **hace**	she makes
usted **es**	you are	usted **hace**	you make
nosotros/as **somos**	we are	nosotros/as **hacemos**	we make
vosotros/as **sois**	you are	vosotros/as **hacéis**	you make
ellos/ellas **son**	they are	ellos/ellas **hacen**	they make
ustedes **son**	you are	ustedes **hacen**	you make

estar	**to be**	**hablar**	**to speak**
yo **estoy**	I am	yo habl**o**	I speak
tú **estás**	you are	tú habl**as**	you speak
él **está**	he is	él habl**a**	he speaks
ella **está**	she is	ella habl**a**	she speaks
usted **está**	you are	usted habl**a**	you speak
nosotros/as **estamos**	we are	nosotros/as habl**amos**	we speak
vosotros/as **estáis**	you are	vosotros/as habl**áis**	you speak
ellos/ellas **están**	they are	ellos/ellas habl**an**	they speak
ustedes **están**	you are	ustedes habl**an**	you speak

In this dictionary, all verbs have examples to show you how to use them.

Index

A, a

abajo: **downstairs**

el abrigo: **coat**

abrir: **open**

acordarse de: **remember**

adiós: **goodbye**

el adulto: **adult**

el aeropuerto: **airport**

el agua *f*: **water**

ahora: **now**

el alfabeto: **alphabet**

alto, alta: **loud, tall**

amable: **kind**

amarillo, amarilla: **yellow**

la ambulancia: **ambulance**

el amigo, la amiga: **friend**

el anillo: **ring**

el animal: **animal**

el año: **year**

antes de: **before**

aprender: **learn**

aquí: **here**

la araña: **spider**

el árbol: **tree**

el arco iris: **rainbow**

la arena: **sand**

arriba: **up, upstairs**

el arroz: **rice**

el autobús: **bus**

el avión (los aviones): **plane**

ayer: **yesterday**

azul: **blue**

B, b

bailar: **dance**

el balón: **ball**

el baño: **bath**

el barco: **boat**

el bebé: **baby**

la bebida: **drink**

el beso: **kiss**

la bicicleta: **bicycle**

bien: **well**

blanco, blanca: **white**

la boca: **mouth**

el bolígrafo: **pen**

el bolsillo: **pocket**

el bolso: **bag**

bonito, bonita: **pretty**

el bosque: **forest**

la bota: **boot**

el brazo: **arm**

la bruja: **witch**

bueno, buena: **good**

C, c

el caballo: **horse**

la cabeza: **head**

la cabra: **goat**

el cachorro: **puppy**

el café: **coffee**

la caja: **box**

el calcetín (los calcetines): **sock**

el calendario: **calendar**

caliente: **hot, warm**

la calle: **road, street**

la cama: **bed**

caminar: **walk**

la camisa: **shirt**

la camiseta: **T-shirt**

el campo: **countryside**

cansado, cansada: **tired**

cantar: **sing**

la cara: **face**

el caracol: **snail**

la carne: **meat**

la carrera: **race**

la carta: **letter**

el cartero: **postman**

la casa: **house**

el castillo: **castle**

la cebra: **zebra**

la cena: **dinner**

el cepillo de dientes: **toothbrush**

la cesta: **basket**

la chaqueta: **jacket**

el chocolate: **chocolate**

el cielo: **sky**

el circo: **circus**

el círculo: **circle**

la ciudad: **town**

el coche: **car**

la cocina: **kitchen**

cocinar: **cook**

coger: **take**

el cohete: **rocket**

el colegio: **school**

los columpios: **playground**

comer: **eat**

la cometa: **kite**

la comida: **food, lunch, meal**

comprar: **buy**

con: **with**

el conejillo de Indias: **guinea pig**

el conejo: **rabbit**

contento, contenta: **happy**

la corbata: **tie**

el cordero: **lamb**

correcto, correcta: **right**

correr: **run**

crecer: **grow**

el cuadrado: **square**

el cubo: **bucket**

la cuchara: **spoon**

el cuchillo: **knife**

el cuerpo: **body**

el cumpleaños (los cumpleaños): **birthday**

D, d

dar: **give**

de: **from, of**

los deberes: **homework**

decir: **say**

el dedo: **finger**

el delfín: **dolphin**

el deporte: **sport**

el desayuno: **breakfast**

el desorden: **mess**

despertarse: **wake up**

después de: **after**

el día: **day**

dibujar: **draw**

el dibujo: **picture**

el diccionario: **dictionary**

el diente: **tooth**

difícil: **difficult**

el dinero: **money**

el dinosaurio: **dinosaur**

el disfraz (los disfraces): **costume**

divertido, divertida: **funny**

dormir: **sleep**

el dragón (los dragones): **dragon**

la ducha: **shower**

duro, dura: **hard**

el DVD (los DVDs): **DVD**

E, e

el ejercicio: **exercise**

el elefante: **elephant**

el email: **email**

encontrar: **find**

encontrarse con: **meet**

el enfermero, la enfermera: **nurse**

enfermo, enferma: **sick**

enseñar: **show**

entender: **understand**

enviar: **send**

el erizo: **hedgehog**

la escalera: **stairs**

esconderse: **hide**

escribir: **write**

escuchar: **listen**

esperar: **wait**

la estación (las estaciones): **station**

la estrella: **star**

el extraterrestre: **alien**

F, f

fácil: **easy**

la falda: **skirt**

la familia: **family**

el fantasma: **ghost**

favorito, favorita: **favourite**

la fiesta: **party**

el fin de semana: **weekend**

la flor: **flower**

la foto: **photo**

el frigorífico: **fridge**

frío, fría: **cold**

la fruta: **fruit**

el fuego: **fire**

los fuegos artificiales: **fireworks**

fuerte: **strong**

el fútbol: **football**

G, g

las gafas: **glasses**

el ganador, la ganadora: **winner**

ganar: **win**

el garaje: **garage**

el gatito: **kitten**

el gato: **cat**

la gente: **people**

el gigante: **giant**

el globo: **balloon**

gracias: **thank you**

grande: **big**

gritar: **shout**

el guante: **glove**

el guisante: **pea**

la guitarra: **guitar**

gustar: **like**

H, h

la habitación (las habitaciones): **bedroom, room**

hablar: **speak, talk**

hacer: **do, make**

la hada: **fairy**

la hamburguesa: **burger**

el hámster (los hámsters): **hamster**

el helado: **ice cream**

el helicóptero: **helicopter**

la hermana: **sister**

el hermano: **brother**

la hierba: **grass**

la hija: **daughter**

el hijo: **son**

la historia: **story**

hola: **hello**

el hombre: **man**

la hora: **hour**

el hospital: **hospital**

hoy: **today**

el huevo: **egg**

I, i

la idea: **idea**

incorrecto, incorrecta: **wrong**

el insecto: **insect**

ir: **go**

la isla: **island**

J, j

el jabón: **soap**

el jardín (los jardines): **garden**

la jirafa: **giraffe**

joven, jóvenes: **young**

el juego: **game**

jugar: **play**

el juguete: **toy**

juntos, juntas: **together**

L, l

el lago: **lake**

la lámpara: **lamp**

el lápiz (los lápices): **pencil**

lavar: **wash**

la leche: **milk**

leer: **read**

lento, lenta: **slow**

el león (los leones): **lion**

el libro: **book**

el limón (los limones): **lemon**

limpio, limpia: **clean**

listo, lista: **ready**

llamar: **call**

la llave: **key**

lleno, llena: **full**

llevar: **wear**

llorar: **cry**

la lluvia: **rain**

Lo siento: **sorry**

el lobo: **wolf**

la luna: **moon**

la luz (las luces): **light**

M, m

la madre: **mother**

el mago: **magician**

malo, mala: **bad**

la mamá: **mum**

la mañana: **morning, tomorrow**

la mano *f*: **hand**

la manta: **blanket**

la mantequilla: **butter**

la manzana: **apple**

el mar: **sea**

el marido: **husband**

la marioneta: **puppet**

la mariposa: **butterfly**

más: **more**

la mascota: **pet**

la medicina: **medicine**

el médico, la médica: **doctor**

menos: **less**

el mensaje de texto: **text message**

el mercado: **market**

la mermelada: **jam**

el mes: **month**

la mesa: **table**

mirar: **look**

mismo, misma: **same**

el mono: **monkey**

el monstruo: **monster**

la montaña: **mountain**

la moqueta: **carpet**

la mosca: **fly**

la moto: **motorbike**

muchos, muchas: **many**

la mujer: **wife, woman**

el mundo: **world**

la muñeca: **doll**

el muñeco de nieve: **snowman**

la música: **music**

muy: **very**

N, n

nada: **nothing**

nadar: **swim**

la nariz (las narices): **nose**

la nave espacial: **spaceship**

necesitar: **need**

negro, negra: **black**

la nieve: **snow**

la niña: **girl**

el niño: **boy**

el niño, la niña: **child, kid**

la noche: **night**

el nombre: **name**

la nube: **cloud**

el número: **number**

O, o

oír: **hear**

el ojo: **eye**

la ola: **wave**

oler: **smell**

el ordenador: **computer**

la oreja: **ear**

el osito de peluche: **teddy bear**

otra vez: **again**

otro, otra: **other**

la oveja: **sheep**

P, p

el padre: **father**

los padres: **parents**

la paga: **pocket money**

la página: **page**

el pájaro: **bird**

la palabra: **word**

los palillos chinos: **chopsticks**

el pan: **bread**

los pantalones: **trousers**

los pantalones cortos: **shorts**

el papá: **dad**

el papel: **paper**

el paraguas (los paraguas): **umbrella**

parar: **stop**

la pared: **wall**

el parque: **park**

el pasaporte: **passport**

la pasta: **pasta**

la pasta de dientes: **toothpaste**

la patata: **potato**

el pato: **duck**

el payaso: **clown**

el pegamento: **glue**

pegar: **stick**

la pegatina: **sticker**

peligroso, peligrosa: **dangerous**

el pelo: **hair**

el peluquero, la peluquera: **hairdresser**

pensar: **think**

pequeño, pequeña: **little**

perder: **lose**

perdido, perdida: **lost**

el periódico: **newspaper**

el perro: **dog**

el pez (los peces): **fish**

el pez de colores (los peces de colores): **goldfish**

el piano: **piano**

el picnic: **picnic**

la piedra: **stone**

la piel: **skin**

la pierna: **leg**

el pijama: **pyjamas**

pintar: **paint**

el/la pirata: **pirate**

la piscina: **swimming pool**

la pizza: **pizza**

la planta: **plant**

el plátano: **banana**

el plato: **plate**

la playa: **beach**

la policía: **police**

el pollo: **chicken**

el póney (los póneys): **pony**

el portátil: **laptop**

la postal: **postcard**

el postre: **dessert**

preguntar: **ask**

primero, primera: **first**

la princesa: **princess**

el príncipe: **prince**

próximo, próxima: **next**

el puente: **bridge**

la puerta: **door**

Q, q

quedarse con: **keep**

querer: **love, want**

el queso: **cheese**

R, r

la radio: **radio**

la radiografía: **X-ray**

la rana: **frog**

rápido, rápida: **fast, quick**

el ratón (los ratones): **mouse**

el regalo: **present**

la reina: **queen**

reírse: **laugh**

el reloj: **clock, watch**

el restaurante: **restaurant**

el rey: **king**

rico, rica: **rich**

el río: **river**

el robot (los robots): **robot**

la rodilla: **knee**

rojo, roja: **red**

el rompecabezas (los rompecabezas): **jigsaw**

la ropa: **clothes**

el ruido: **noise**

S, s

saber: **know**

saltar: **jump**

salvaje: **wild**

el sándwich: **sandwich**

segundo, segunda: **second**

la semana: **week**

la señora: **lady**

sentarse: **sit**

la serpiente: **snake**

el servicio: **toilet**

la silla: **chair**

la silla de ruedas: **wheelchair**

la sillita de paseo: **pushchair**

simpático, simpática: **nice**

sin: **without**

la sirena: **mermaid**

el sitio web: **website**

el sofá: **sofa**

el sol: **sun**

la sombra: **shadow**

el sombrero: **hat**

la sonrisa: **smile**

la sopa: **soup**

la sorpresa: **surprise**

sucio, sucia: **dirty**

el suelo: **floor, ground**

el sueño: **dream**

el supermercado: **supermarket**

T, t

la tarde: **afternoon, evening**

la tarjeta: **card**

la tarta: **cake**

el taxi: **taxi**

el té: **tea**

el teléfono: **telephone**

la televisión: **television**

el tenedor: **fork**

tener: **have**

tercero, tercera: **third**

el tesoro: **treasure**

la tienda: **shop**

la Tierra: **Earth**

el tigre: **tiger**

las tijeras: **scissors**

la toalla: **towel**

todos, todas: **every**

el tomate: **tomato**

la tortuga: **tortoise**

las tostadas: **toast**

trabajar: **work**

el trabajo: **job**

el tractor: **tractor**

traer: **bring**

tranquilo, tranquila: **quiet**

el tren: **train**

el triángulo: **triangle**

triste: **sad**

U, u

único, única: **only**

el uniforme: **uniform**

las uvas: **grapes**

V, v

la vaca: **cow**

las vacaciones: **holiday**

vacío, vacía: **empty**

la vainilla: **vanilla**

los vaqueros: **jeans**

el vaso: **glass**

el vecino, la vecina: **neighbour**

la vela: **candle**

vender: **sell**

venir: **come**

la ventana: **window**

ver: **see**

la verdura: **vegetable**

el vestido: **dress**

el veterinario, la veterinaria: **vet**

el videojuego: **video game**

viejo, vieja: **old**

el viento: **wind**

visitar: **visit**

vivir: **live**

W, w

la webcam (las webcams): **webcam**

X, x

el xilófono: **xylophone**

Y, y

y: **and**

Z, z

la zanahoria: **carrot**

el zapato: **shoe**

el zoo: **zoo**

el zumo: **juice**